RATS ON THE ROOF

and Other Stories

JAMES MARSHALL

HOUGHTON MIFFLIN   BOSTON • MORRIS PLAINS, NJ

California • Colorado • Georgia • Illinois • New Jersey • Texas

To Victoria Roberts

CONTENTS

Rats on
the Roof

Otis and Sophie Dog had just tucked themselves in for the night when the sound of little dancing feet and shrill musical instruments reached their sleepy ears.

"Oh no!" cried Otis. "We've got rats on the roof!"

"It looks like we're in for it," Sophie said, pulling up the comforter and sticking her head under the pillow. Otis Dog did the same.

"I'll think of something in the morning," he said. "This will call for some drastic measures."

It was a long and sleepless night. The

racket on the roof had not let up, and in the morning the Dogs were tired. They discussed the situation over breakfast.

"We shall simply have to get a cat," said Otis. Sophie set down her coffee cup.

"Oh my," she said. "Has it come to *that*? You know how difficult cats can be."

"There's nothing else to be done," said her husband. "I'll place an advertisement in the newspaper today."

"I hope you know what you're doing," said Sophie.

Three mornings later the Dogs were more tired than ever. The nightly commotion had gotten worse, and no one had responded to the newspaper ad. Otis Dog, his paws shaking from lack of sleep, could barely get his toast to his mouth.

"We may have to move," he said. The doorbell rang, and the Dogs jumped up from the breakfast table.

"Hurry, hurry!" cried Sophie. Rushing into the entrance hall, they threw open the front door. A large orange tomcat stood before them.

"You advertised for a cat?" he asked.

"Indeed we did!" said Otis Dog. "We really need a cat."

"Everybody does," said the tomcat, nonchalantly stepping over the threshold. "Cats simply *make* a home."

"When can you begin?" asked Sophie.

"Let's not be premature," said the tomcat. "There are a few questions to be addressed. First of all, where would I sleep? Cats do a lot of that, you know."

"Well," said Sophie, quickly improvising, "we could put some rags in the hall closet or perhaps behind the stove."

"You *are* amusing," said the tomcat, strolling into the living room and looking about.

"This sofa will do nicely. I'm fond of crushed velvet. And that big overstuffed armchair looks comfy, although we'll have to do something about that ghastly color."

"My favorite armchair," muttered Otis under his breath.

"And then there is the matter of my

meals," continued the tomcat, casually running his paw along the piano to inspect for dust. "I require three squares a day plus snacks in the late afternoon. I like a varied menu and I insist on fixed hours. I tend to get irritable when I'm made to wait."

"Now see here!" said Sophie.

The tomcat looked surprised. "You did say you needed a *cat,* didn't you?"

"Yes, oh yes!" said Otis, giving his wife a look. "I'm sure we'll have no trouble meeting your requirements."

Sophie Dog bit her lip.

"And finally there is the little matter of my salary," said the tomcat.

"Salary?" said the Dogs.

"Of *course,*" said the tomcat. "All cats receive a salary. Didn't you know that? Mine is ten dollars a week. I usually receive more, but because this is such a pleasant house, I'm giving you a reduced rate."

The Dogs looked at each other. "Ten dollars a week is a considerable sum," said Otis. "I'd like to discuss this with my wife, if you don't mind."

"By all means," said the tomcat, who

looked as if he didn't care one way or the other. "You don't want to make any hasty decisions."

The Dogs stepped onto the sun porch.

"Really!" said Sophie. "Of all the nerve!"

"I tell you it's the only way," said Otis. "Once he disposes of our little problem, he can go." Sophie was skeptical.

"But ten dollars a week!"

"It will be worth it for a good night's sleep," said her husband. "I will take full responsibility."

Sophie let her husband have his way, and they stepped back into the living room.

"You're hired," said Otis Dog.

"Splendid," said the tomcat. "I'll send for my things."

"We should discuss your duties," said Sophie, getting to the point. The tomcat seemed not to understand.

"Duties?" he said. "You mean a cat's duty to add grace and elegance to the surroundings? Have no fear of that."

"That's not what I had in mind."

"Then you must be thinking of our educational value," said the tomcat. "I'm told that cat-watching can be highly instructive."

"Yes, yes," said Sophie. "That's all very nice. But actually I was referring to the little problem we have with some rats."

"Come again?" said the tomcat.

"We have rats on our roof," said Sophie Dog. "They're extremely noisy, and they've been keeping us up night after night."

"You *did* say rats!" cried the tomcat. "Rats! I can't *stand* it!" And he went quite off his head—tearing from room to room, climbing the walls, knocking over the furniture, banging on the piano. He went from window to window, sticking his head out and screaming at the top of his voice. "They've got RATS in here! Somebody *do* something! Call 911! Ooh! Ugh! How disgusting! I can't stand their beedy little eyes, those nasty skinny tails, those dirty little nails!"

Without even saying good-bye, the deranged tomcat crashed through the screen door, tore across the front lawn, and disappeared down the street.

"I'm glad so many of our neighbors are out of town," said Otis Dog.

"I told you cats can be difficult," said his wife.

That night the Dogs were surprised to find a handwritten note on their bedside table. The note read as follows:

To Whom It May Concern,

Owing to the excessively noisy disruption of our daytime sleeping schedule, we find ourselves no longer able to remain in residence. We are leaving.

Signed,
The Rats on the Roof

"Well, I'll be," said Sophie Dog.

"Fancy that," said her husband. And they climbed into bed, pulled up the comforter, and went right to sleep.

They would sleep until noon.

A Sheepish Tale

One afternoon two sheep decided to be wild and daring and go for an unsupervised walk.

"We can take care of ourselves," said Fred.

"Of course we can," said Monty.

Before long they found themselves at the edge of a forest.

"I wonder what that sign says," said Fred. "I can't read."

"I can! I can read!" said Monty. "I read all the time!"

His friend looked at him. "*You* can read? *You?* Prove it! What does it say?"

Monty squinted at the sign.

"Well," he said. "For your information, it says, 'Welcome to the pretty green forest.' "

Fred was impressed. "You *can* read!" he said.

And the two of them entered the forest.

Within no time they were in the deepest, dampest part.

"Isn't this fun?" said Monty.

"It's wild!" exclaimed Fred. "But look —there's another sign. What does it say?"

Monty squinted. "It says, 'Help Prevent Forest Fires.' "

"Very sensible," said Fred.
And they continued on.

When they came to a fork in the path
and two small signs, Fred said, "Well?"

"This sign says 'This Way' and that
one says 'That Way,'" said Monty.

"You're *so* smart!" said Fred.
And they went that way.

Soon they arrived at a little house.

"I wonder if anyone lives in there," said Fred.

Inside the house, which was rundown and unkempt, a wolf was thinking about food.

"I've eaten just about everything in the forest, and now there's nothing left," he said. "I'm being cruelly punished."

Suddenly he smelled something delightful; and rushing to the window, he could scarcely believe his eyes.

"What's this?" he cried. "I must be dreaming!"

"Yoo hoo!" called out the two sheep. "Anybody home?"

"I'm coming!" the wolf called back. "I just have to throw on some clothes."

And with his heart racing, he rummaged about for something to disguise himself.

"If they see me, they'll hightail it away. And I'm not nearly so fast as I used to be."

At the back of a cupboard, he found a musty old sheepskin.

"Excellent," he said. "I'll pounce as soon as they are in the door."

But an unpleasant thought occurred to him. What if while he was pouncing on one sheep, the other managed to escape? That would really be *too* awful. And then a clever solution came to him. If both sheep were *sleeping,* he'd have a much easier time of it. Yes, that was it. It would require a bit of waiting and self-discipline, but it would be well worth it.

Outside, the sheep were getting restless.

"Shh," said Fred. "I hear someone coming. Maybe we'll get ourselves invited to dinner."

The door opened.

Standing before them was a large sheep, not unlike themselves.

"Welcome, my friends," said the large sheep. "And come in."

The two sheep stepped over the threshold.

The wolf got right to the point. "You will of course stay the night," he said.

"Evening is coming, and there are wolves just everywhere."

"Wolves!" cried the two sheep.

"Yes," said their host, nodding his head sadly, "but you will be safe here. In the morning you can slip away. Wolves, I believe, are late sleepers."

The sheep were most grateful and said so. "Lucky for us we ran into you," said Monty.

"Lucky indeed," said the wolf.

While waiting for night to fall, the wolf served the sheep some weak tea and sat down at the table. He tried to appear interested in what the sheep had to say.

"Did you hear what happened to old Farmer Jones?" said Fred. "He tripped over Bossy's bucket."

"He *didn't*!" said Monty.

"He *did*."

"My, my," said the wolf.

"Farmer Smith has a new tractor," said Monty.

"How many cylinders?" said Fred.

"Two," said Monty. "No, four."

The wolf drummed his paws on the table.

"Don't drink too much tea. It could keep you awake," he said.

"And did you hear about Farmer Johnson's dog?" said Fred. "She had puppies."

"She *didn't*!" said Monty.

"She *did*!"

Finally, the poor wolf couldn't stand it any longer. His eyelids were getting heavy. A catnap would restore his energy.

In a moment he was snoring away.

"And *then* Farmer Jones's chickens all caught the chicken pox . . ." Fred was saying. But he didn't finish.

The host's snoring became quite raucous and he began to twitch in his sleep. His mouth opened in a tremendous gaping yawn and the sheepskin fell to the floor.

"A wolf!" whispered the sheep.

And tiptoeing out of the house, they hit the front path running and did not stop until they were clear out of the forest.

When the wolf awoke several hours later, he looked about and saw that he was entirely alone.

"It must have been a dream after all," he said. "Too good to be true."

The Mouse
Who Got Married

Early one morning in May, a mouse sprang out of bed, danced into the bathroom, and stepped under an ice-cold shower.

"Tra-la!" he sang, soaping up his whiskers. "Today is my wedding day!"

In another part of town, a large tomcat was reading the morning paper and filing his claws. Rather bored with the news of the day, he turned to the wedding page, just to see if any of his friends had taken the plunge. One particular item arrested his attention.

Mr. and Mrs. Grover T. Mousewood of 93 Cheddar Lane announce the engagement of their daughter Mary Louise to Mr. Cedric Mousejoy of 35 Stilton Street. The nuptials will take place this afternoon at St. Michael's. A reception will follow in the parish hall.

"Now this *is* news!" said the tomcat. "A whole church full of mice! Mice, I do believe, have large families."

For the rest of the morning the tomcat could only think of one thing—and it wasn't at all pretty.

"I must get into that church!" he said. "I must!"

But then he had another idea.

"No," he said, scratching his chin, "I think I'll wait for the reception, when everyone is good and stuffed."

At 35 Stilton Street, Cedric Mousejoy put a flower in his buttonhole and admired himself in a full-length mirror.

"I'll be marrying the most splendid mouse in the world!" he sang at the top of his lungs. "Even if she is on the tall side, we'll make a fine couple."

He stood on tiptoe to give himself some extra height.

"Little things like that don't matter when you're in love," he said.

The doorbell rang and Cedric opened the door to find his best man Bob trembling on the steps.

"I'm so nervous," said Bob. "What if something should go wrong?"

"What could possibly go wrong?" said Cedric.

The tomcat, now quite famished, adjusted his cravat and admired himself in the mirror.

"Excellent," he said. "Excellent."

"I can't believe my eyes," said his old

mother from the next room. "Does this mean you are actually going to church?"

"In a manner of speaking," said the tomcat, and he divulged his plans for a big Sunday dinner.

"Of course," he said, "I'll bring you a nice big piece of cake."

"You *are* dense!" snapped his mother. "I see you haven't learned anything! Those mice will see you coming a mile away. You'll never get inside."

The tomcat suddenly felt deflated. He saw that once again his old mother was right, and he sat down on the sofa and sobbed.

"But I had my heart set on it!" he cried.

"There, there," said his mother. "All is not lost. I'll think of something."

It was a beautiful ceremony. The altar of St. Michael's was banked with lilacs, and

the scent was heavenly. The mother of the bride dabbed her eyes with a hankie and sighed. The best man did not forget the ring, and the happy couple said their "I do's" loud and clear. A reception followed in the parish hall.

"That's odd," said Grover T. Mousewood, the father of the bride, "I don't remember ordering a cake so big. How much does that thing cost?"

"Oh hush," said his wife. "Don't be such an old tightwad. It's Mary Louise's wedding. Be happy!"

"Oh, I am, I am!" said her husband.

After a sumptuous meal of imported cheese casseroles, it was time for the bride and groom to cut the cake.

"Are you ready?" said Cedric to the photographer.

"Ready when you are!" called out the photographer. "Cut the cake!"

Suddenly out of the cake, before the astonished eyes of the wedding party, leapt the tomcat. Little bits of frosting stuck to his ears and tail, and there was a terrible look in his yellow eyes.

"I've got you now!" he cried, looking around for his first course.

The frightened guests all backed up against the wall. Several of them fainted straightaway.

"We're done for!" said the best man Bob.

"Now just one little minute," someone said.

The tomcat spun around to find himself facing the largest mouse he'd ever seen in his life.

"Nobody is going to spoil *my* wedding day!" shouted Mary Louise. "Nobody!"

And without further ado, she picked the tomcat up by the scruff of his neck and tossed him through the front door into the street, where he landed with an awful thud.

"And take this with you!" cried Mary Louise, hurling the giant cake after him.

The next morning at breakfast the tomcat came across this very interesting announcement in the newspaper:

Miss Mary Louise Mousewood and Mr. Cedric Mousejoy were married yesterday in a solemn ceremony at St. Michael's. A reception followed in the parish hall. The couple is now honeymooning in Boston.

"Rats!" said the tomcat. "There is no mention of me whatsoever."

"Just as well," said his mother. "Have another piece of cake. We have plenty."

Meanwhile, on the terrace of their hotel in Boston, Mr. and Mrs. Cedric Mousejoy were discussing their wedding day in detail.

"Too bad that dreadful cat had to crash the party," said Cedric.

"Don't worry, dear," said his wife. "Life is full of unpleasant little surprises.

But together we'll manage to rise above
them."

And Cedric Mousejoy knew he had
indeed married the most splendid mouse
in the world.

Eat Your Vegetables

An owl, who had decided to spend the morning in bed, was fluffing up her pillows when she heard the most awful noise from outside. It was the sound of munching. And it was coming closer.

"Termites!" cried the owl. "They must be gigantic!"

But when she stepped out her front door, she saw what was up. And it wasn't termites. A brontosaurus was merrily eating the oak tree in which the owl made her home.

"Delicious," said the brontosaurus. "I really think I prefer oak to elm. Although an occasional hickory is a nice alternative."

"May I ask what you think you are doing?" said the owl.

"I'm having my breakfast," replied the brontosaurus calmly. "*If* you don't mind."

"I *do* mind," said the owl. "This is my home. Go find breakfast someplace else."

"I'll do no such thing," said the brontosaurus. "You'll simply have to relocate."

And he opened his ferocious jaws and took another bite.

"That's my terrace!" shrieked the owl. "I'm warning you!"

The brontosaurus found this amusing.

"Oh yes?" he said. "Just what do you intend to do about it?"

"You'll see," said the owl.

And she hurried inside to make emergency calls to all her friends.

"Stop everything and get over here at once!" she cried. "There isn't a second to lose!"

The brontosaurus didn't give the owl
another thought and continued with his
breakfast. He hummed a little tune as he
chewed. Suddenly he heard the sound of
flapping wings. Before he knew it, the oak
tree was covered with birds—sparrows and

larks, hawks, gulls and crows, finches, hummingbirds, buzzards and canaries. They were perched on every branch. They looked defiant.

"Out of my way!" roared the brontosaurus.

But the owl's friends would not budge. The brontosaurus tried to find an empty branch to nibble on, but everywhere he looked a bird was stationed.

"You'll have to eat *us* along with the leaves and branches," said the owl.

"Ugh!" cried the brontosaurus. "What a disgusting thought. You *know* I'm a vegetarian!"

"I'm nice and bitter," said one of the crows.

"I'm on the slimy side myself," said a pigeon.

The brontosaurus felt his stomach turning a little queasy.

"I'm good and salty," said a plump gull.

"Stop that!" roared the brontosaurus.

"I hope you don't mind a few bones with your buzzard," said one old bird.

By now the brontosaurus felt positively nauseated. But although his appetite was ruined, he didn't want to lose face.

"I believe I hear someone calling me," he said. "We'll continue this discussion some other time."

And he lumbered away and out of sight.

"Nice work," said the owl to the other birds.

"Some problems we just can't manage alone," said the buzzard. "And it's wonderful to have friends to whom we can turn in a crunch."

"You said a mouthful," said the owl.

Swan Song

A cow was waiting at the bus stop minding her own business, when a frightened swan ran up to her.

"Help! Help!" cried the swan. "A fox is after me!"

"Oh dear," said the cow. "That's not good."

"*Do* something!" cried the swan.

"Now calm down," said the cow. "I will help, but you must do *exactly* as I say."

A moment later a panting fox rounded the corner and skidded to a halt.

"Pardon me, madam," he said, bowing low to the cow. "Did you by any chance see a swan pass this way?"

"Why do you ask?" said the cow.

"Er," said the fox. "She's a friend of mine, and I have a present for her."

"No," replied the cow. "I did not see your friend."

The fox scratched his chin.

"Well, thanks all the same," he said. "And by the way, that is an exquisite hat you are wearing."

"Thank you," said the cow. "It is new."

"Ha, ha, ha!" sang out the swan. "It's not a hat at all! It's *me*! We fooled you! We fooled you!"

"Aha!" cried the fox.

And he leapt up and tried to snatch the swan from atop the cow's head.

"Hold on tight!" called out the cow.

And with that she pulled up her skirts and tore off down the road at a tremendous clip, leaving behind the wicked fox

coughing and wheezing in a cloud of dust.
He was absolutely furious.

When they had gotten a safe distance
away, the cow put the swan down.

"You did not keep quiet as I in-
structed," said the cow.

"Well my heavens," said the swan. "I
had to show that fox how smart we are."

"Sometimes being *really* smart is knowing when to say nothing," said the cow. "But I see that I was all wrong about you. I mistook you for a swan, when you are nothing but a silly goose."

Ooh-La-La

My goodness me," said a young frog, catching sight of his reflection in a shop window. "I have never noticed it before, but I have *magnificent* legs!"

"Vanity, vanity," chirped a sparrow.

"Well I *do*!" said the frog.

And feeling quite pleased with himself, he hopped on down the street. In the middle of the next block, he paused to buy a newspaper from a rabbit friend.

"Look at these," said the frog. "Aren't they just about the most glorious legs you've ever seen?"

"Huh?" said the rabbit, who was sure he'd misunderstood.

"I knew you'd think so," said the frog.

And he took his newspaper and disappeared around the corner. Soon he saw
a possum friend busily hanging out her
laundry. Tiptoeing up behind a wet blan-
ket, the frog exhibited first one leg and then
the other.

"What do you think of *these*?" he said
to the possum. "Aren't they the most
stunning legs you've ever laid eyes on?"

"They certainly are," said the possum, who was sure the frog was joking.

"Now I'm off to sit by the pond," said the frog. "I so enjoy reading my morning paper in peace and quiet."

And he hopped on down the road leading out of town. Soon he ran into an old collie friend.

"I see you can't help noticing my legs," said the frog.

"Beg pardon?" said the collie.

"My legs," said the frog. "Aren't they the most wonderful legs you've ever seen in your life?"

"Er . . . quite," said the collie, who thought for sure the frog had gone completely insane. "Very fine legs indeed. So green, so slimy."

"And now I'm off to sit by the pond and read my newspaper," said the frog. "Ta-ta."

"Ta-ta," said the collie, shaking his head sadly as the frog hopped away.

At the pond, the young frog found a large, sunny boulder, stretched out upon it, and opened his morning paper for a nice long read. As the news of the day was unusually dull, he turned to the Home Section. After skimming various articles, he finally came to one that seemed of interest. It was titled, "Magnificent Frog Legs," by Madame Cecile.

"Must be some beauty tips," said the frog. "Not that *I* need any."

"The French, as everyone knows, are the supreme masters when it comes to the preparation of frog legs," wrote Madame Cecile. "By far the most popular recipe is that of sautéing the frog legs in lots of butter, garlic, and herbs. Ooh-la-la!"

The young frog's eyes nearly popped out of his head.

"Egads!" he cried.

And he hopped back to town as fast as he could.

"Forget what I was saying earlier!" he called out, overtaking the collie. "My legs are simply *covered* in green bumps and unsightly blotches. Spread it around."

He hurried on.

"Poor thing," said the collie. "He's getting worse."

"I was only joking about my legs," said the frog to the possum. "No need to repeat what I said."

"Oh, I knew you were joking," said the possum.

"Legs? Did you think I said something about *legs*?" cried the frog to the rabbit. "Ha ha! I said I need to purchase some *eggs*! Grade A *eggs*! Forget I said anything at all."

"I was sure I hadn't heard correctly," said the rabbit.

The young frog hurried home to look for a pair of long, unattractive woolen socks. But before he could enter his little house, he bumped into a French poodle who had recently moved into the neighborhood.

"Bonjour," said the poodle, tipping his beret.

"Oh no!" screamed the frog.

And he ran inside and bolted the door.

"I will never be vain again!" he cried. "Never, never, never!"

His words resounded from room to room.

"My goodness me," said the frog. "I've never noticed it before, but I have a *beautiful* voice."

Miss Jones

Miss Jones had just settled down to a mug of milky tea and a plate of crackers, when the telephone rang.

"I might have known," she complained. "Someone always calls when I'm having treats."

Miss Jones waddled over to the telephone and picked up the receiver.

"Hello," she said, somewhat irritably.

"Well?" said her friend Rose, who lived in the building. "What are they like, your new neighbors across the hall in 12E? The postman said a couple moved in during the night."

"I haven't heard a thing," said Miss

Jones, "but my hearing isn't what it used to be."

"I'm dying to know what they look like," said Rose. "Why don't you peek out into the hall and see what you can see?"

"You know how dark that hall is," said Miss Jones, "and besides, my eyesight isn't so good. I can't see my beak in front of my face."

"Well as soon as you hear anything at all, give me a call," said Rose. And she hung up.

Miss Jones nibbled on her crackers and sipped her milky tea.

"New neighbors," she said. "I do hope we get along."

When she had finished her snack, she took the dishes into the kitchen to wash up.

"Moving is such hard work," she said, "I think I'll heat up some vegetable soup and take it over. That will be a friendly gesture."

When the soup was ready, Miss Jones stepped across the hall. It took her some time to locate the bell.

"Who is it?" called out a deep female voice.

"It is Miss Jones from across the hall," said Miss Jones. "I've brought you some vegetable soup."

The door of 12E opened, but just a crack.

Miss Jones could not see the long furry nose protruding out, or the long, sharp white teeth.

"I thought you might be too tired to cook," said Miss Jones.

"We *can't* cook yet," said the new neighbor. "The gas company hasn't turned on the gas. Otherwise . . ."

"Well then," said Miss Jones, holding

out the pot of soup, "I hope you'll enjoy
this."

"Thanks," said the new neighbor.

Miss Jones squinted and stepped closer
to the open door.

"I really can't see you very well," she
said, "this hallway is so dark."

"My husband and I are canaries," said
the new neighbor quickly.

"Oh, how lovely," said Miss Jones. "But you don't sound like canaries."

"We have low voices," said the neighbor.

"But we *are* canaries," said a deep male voice from behind the door. "We are the Carusos."

"I'm so pleased to meet you," said Miss Jones. "When you are all settled in, we must get together for dinner."

The Carusos both gasped.

"By all means!" said Mrs. Caruso. "We'd like nothing better."

"I'll be off now," said Miss Jones. "Toodleloo."

"Toodleloo," said the Carusos.

Miss Jones went inside her apartment. Charming couple, she thought.

Mrs. Caruso closed the door to 12E. "If only that stove had been working!" she said.

That evening Miss Jones consulted her calendar.

"My stars," she said. "Christmas is only two days away. I really must start planning my big Christmas dinner."

But then she remembered that this Christmas her friend Rose would be out of town visiting her family.

"It will be a lonely Christmas indeed," said Miss Jones. "But I'll make the best of it."

The doorbell rang.

"Who is it?" called out Miss Jones, who never opened the door without knowing who was on the other side.

"It is I, Mrs. Caruso," said the new neighbor.

Miss Jones threw open the door. "Do come in," she said.

"I only have a minute," said Mrs. Caruso, remaining in the dark hall. "My husband and I were hoping you'd join us for Christmas dinner. It would give us such pleasure."

Miss Jones was thrilled.

"I should be delighted!" she exclaimed. "May I bring anything?"

"Just yourself," said Mrs. Caruso, and she hurried back into her own apartment.

"What a lovely surprise," said Miss Jones, closing and bolting her door.

The next morning the telephone rang.

"Well?" said Rose. "Have you met them yet?"

"Oh yes," said Miss Jones. "They are delightful. Canaries, you know. And they have invited me for Christmas dinner."

"Marvelous," said Rose. "Now I don't have to worry about you being all alone."

No sooner had Miss Jones hung up the telephone than it rang again.

It was Mrs. Caruso. "I hate to bother you, my dear," she said, "but do you by any chance have a nice big roasting pan? Ours seems to have gotten lost in the move."

"Why certainly," said Miss Jones. "Is there anything else you need?"

"As a matter of fact," said Mrs. Caruso, "would you know a good recipe for plum sauce?"

"I surely do," replied Miss Jones. "And why don't you allow me to make it? I'd so love to contribute to the dinner."

"If you like," said Mrs. Caruso.

There was a short pause.

"I *do* hope I don't ruin the wild rice again this year," said Mrs. Caruso.

Miss Jones insisted on preparing the wild rice as well. "I'd be happy to do it," she said. "You just concentrate on the main course."

"Oh we will," said Mrs. Caruso.

Miss Jones felt it would be impolite to ask what the main course would be. "I'm sure it will bc tasty."

On Christmas Eve Mrs. Caruso called again with a slight problem.

"The gas company still hasn't turned on the stove," she said. "I don't know *what* we're going to do!"

Miss Jones had the solution immediately.

"But you must use mine," she said.

"You are kind. What would we do without you?" said Mrs. Caruso. "Have the oven good and hot about noon."

"We can have eggnog while we're waiting for dinner," said Miss Jones.

Mrs. Caruso thought this was an excellent idea, although she confessed that eggnog was really not one of her specialties.

On Christmas morning the Carusos were up bright and early.

"This is going to be a Christmas to remember!" said Mr. Caruso.

"Yum, yum, yum!" said his wife. "I hope there will be plenty of plum sauce."

In her own apartment, Miss Jones, who had gotten up even earlier, was merrily setting the table.

"I have such pretty china," she said.

At noon on the nose, the Carusos rang the doorbell, and Miss Jones opened the door.

"Merry Christmas!" she said.

"Merry Christmas!" said the Carusos, stepping inside. "Is the oven nice and hot?"

"Oh dear, oh dear," said Miss Jones. "I *knew* I'd forget something."

The Carusos were quite put out, but they tried not to show it.

"No harm done," said Mrs. Caruso. "Turn it on right now. We'll start on the eggnog."

Miss Jones went into the kitchen and came back shortly.

"It won't take long to heat up," she said.

"Good," said the Carusos.

Conversation did not flow easily.

"Nice day," said Mr. Caruso.

"Very nice indeed," said Miss Jones, "and so lovely to share it with new neighbors."

"Yes," said the Carusos.

"I think I'll go see about the oven," said Mrs. Caruso, and she got up to go into the kitchen. Suddenly Miss Jones felt a long furry tail brush up against her feet as Mrs. Caruso passed.

Oh no, thought Miss Jones, the Carusos aren't canaries at all!

And right away she saw what was up.

"Miss Jones, dear," Mrs. Caruso called out from the kitchen. "Would you step in here a minute?"

Miss Jones knew she had to do some fast talking—or else!

"I'm sure you can take care of everything," she answered back. "You don't need me. Come have another cup of eggnog."

Mrs. Caruso returned.

"The oven is ready," she said, giving her husband a significant look.

"I'm sure I won't be able to eat more than a few bites," said Miss Jones. "Ever since my operation I haven't had much appetite."

"Operation?" said the Carusos.

"Actually, I've had several," said Miss Jones. "They took out my gizzard."

"Not the gizzard!" said Mr. Caruso, who'd always been partial to gizzards.

"And I have only a tiny bit of my liver left," said Miss Jones. "Hardly anything at all."

"That's really too bad!" said the Carusos.

"Of course," said Miss Jones, "my doctor does want me to put on weight. I'm just a bag of bones."

"You look pretty plump to me," said Mrs. Caruso.

"Feathers," said Miss Jones. "Merely feathers, very deceptive."

The Carusos could now see their big Christmas dinner vanishing before their very eyes.

Miss Jones began to scratch frantically.

"Do excuse me," she said. "I know it's rude to do this in company, but I have such a flea problem."

"You don't say," said the Carusos.

Miss Jones continued.

"Of course," she said, "I'm not implying I don't have absolute faith in my doctor, but I do wish he wouldn't give me all that medicine. I'm positively *stuffed* with milk of magnesia."

Now this was simply too much for the Carusos, and they hastily made their excuses.

"We hate to run off like this," said Mr. Caruso, "but we forgot we always visit shut-ins at Christmastime."

Miss Jones did not insist on their staying.

"We'll get together in the new year," she said.

"Of course," said the Carusos (if that was their real name), and they hurried off, hoping to find *something* decent to eat for Christmas.

"You and your bright ideas!" mumbled Mr. Caruso.

Miss Jones bolted the door, collapsed on the sofa, and heaved great sighs of relief. Then she placed a call to her landlord, who was shocked to learn he had wolves in the building.

"I shall remedy this situation immediately, Miss Jones," he said.

Miss Jones felt reassured and vowed

to open her door to no one until she was advised that the Carusos had departed for good.

That night she sat down to a big plate of plum sauce.

"I really shouldn't," she said. "My doctor says I'm a little overweight, but sometimes we need to reward ourselves."

And she ate it all.

About the Author

James Marshall (1942–1992), a 1989 Caldecott Honor winner, is world famous for such classics as the George and Martha books, his fairy tale retellings, and the Stupids books, as well as two Easy-to-Read™ series—one featuring frisky Fox and the other the Three by the Sea gang. James Marshall's last book was *Rats on the Range*, which is the sequel to *Rats on the Roof*.